MASTER HMO'S TODAY,
CHANGE YOUR LIFE
FOREVER

A COMPENDIUM OF HMO DADDY'S BLOGS

'BASED ON TOPICS I AM ASKED'

By C. J. Haliburton, the leading writer, trainer and
authority on how to multi-let property

HMO Daddy
14 Walsall Road
Wednesbury
West Midlands
WS10 9JL

Print Edition
British Library Cataloguing in Publication Data.
A catalogue record for this book is available from the British Library.
Cover design and formatting by Oxford Literary Consultancy

MASTER HMO'S TODAY,
CHANGE YOUR LIFE
FOREVER

CONTENTS

MASTER HMO'S TODAY,
CHANGE YOUR LIFE
FOREVER

WARNING

Jim Haliburton, known as the HMO Daddy, is not a lawyer or financial advisor, nor does the following represent legal or financial advice. If such advice is needed then the reader should seek professional guidance from qualified experts with appropriate public liability insurance. The following information is given to the best of Jim Haliburton's knowledge and is provided for educational purposes only. It is the reader's responsibility to obtain their own professional advice.

ACKNOWLEDGEMENT

Welcome to *A Compendium of HMO Daddy's Blogs*. My aim is to inform other HMO landlords and those who are considering entering the market of the problems and issues that surround running an HMO. I hope you will not find the blogs too difficult to understand, that my explanations are clear, and that you will be alerted to the problems and issues involved. The blogs are a result of the issues that I am asked about and I cannot help giving my opinion. If you like what you read, there are over forty more issues in *HMO Daddy Reveals All*, available from www.hmodaddy.com.

This business can be a lonely road with seemingly no one to turn who is able to understand the problems we encounter. Getting impartial advice has always been difficult, as those who are in the know and disseminate information usually have an agenda, which is normally to sell you something. Information is all that distinguishes the expert from the ignorant and, as we know, a high price can be charged for this. The "experts" will either want to create a dependency or charge a good price for their expertise, and I am not knocking them for that. I would be a hypocrite to do so, as I also provide courses, books, mentorships and consultancy myself. However, I have not held back and have told it as I believe it, and where extra information is genuinely needed I have said so. I have yet to understand why so few believe me. It is not as if I do not 'walk to the talk'.

I have been an HMO landlord for over 25 years; I now have over 140 HMOs and over 900 tenants, yet those who have no or very few HMOs tell me I cannot do what I do! So-called experts question what I do. The worst culprit is commercial finance.

If I had £1,000 for each time I was told 'you cannot get commercial financing for HMOs' I would have an extra million, or in my case, a pile more property. Perhaps someone will explain to me one day why so few believe me. I am not upset, just curious.

We are often vilified by the press and the chattering classes, not to mention the unreasonable persecution by some Local Authority Housing Standards departments, whose efforts could be used more productively by looking at their own appalling housing. It is a very unfair life being an HMO landlord, but the risks and benefits are yours for the taking.

The journey may be hard, but there is light at the end of the tunnel. With housing price inflation, you should make a good return on selling up, though I do not think that would be a sensible thing to do – after all, why leave a business which becomes increasingly more profitable?

I would like to thank Kelly Munroe for helping me select the topics, Toni Neal for typing up numerous manuscripts, and Hannah Moodie, Rachel Tonks, Will Donaldson, Piers Benton among others for their proofreading and comments. Last but not least, I would like to thank my family and my dog who give me sanity.

C. J. Haliburton
September 2017

ABOUT JIM HALIBURTON
THE AUTHOR

Jim started in property in 1991. He was a college lecturer letting a house to students and slowly built up a small portfolio of student lets. This changed in 1995 when he lost most of his students, as the college changed the way it advertised accommodation. He then started to let to mostly working tenants and continued to grow a portfolio of HMOs, also known as shared houses or multi-lets. He now has over 140 HMOs. After leaving his job as a lecturer in 2004, he continued his passion for lecturing and started to lecture on HMOs. In 2005, Jim wrote *A Guide to Becoming a Multi-Millionaire HMO Landlord*, still the leading manual on the subject. He is in demand as a speaker on the property circuit, runs courses and mentorships and has written many books on the subject of being an HMO landlord and how to acquire property. He still runs courses and mentorships and is available for private consultations.

He has published the following manuals, guides and books:

A Guide to Becoming a Multi-Millionaire HMO Landlord

Operating Standards for HMO Landlords

DIY Eviction – a guide on how to legally, quickly and cheaply evict tenants

Forms, Notices and Letters for HMO Landlords

35 Money Making or Saving Tips for HMO Landlords

The Rules for HMO Landlords

Planning and HMOs

Cases for HMO Landlords on Unlawful and Illegal Eviction

A HMO Daddy Reveals All

A Guide to Letting to the Unemployed

101 Questions and Answers for HMO Landlords

Even More 101 Questions and Answers for HMO Landlords

All available from his website www.hmodaddy.com.

INTRODUCTION

This is the third book I have written because of reader demand, the first being *101 Questions and Answers on HMOs*, and the other being *Current Issues for HMO Landlords*. These books consist entirely of topics readers have asked me about. Previously, I wrote books and manuals for my staff and on topics I thought would be of interest to readers.

I hope this book provides some help in understanding more about this business, though I suspect it may have the opposite effect in that there is often no answer. But at least you know this by now. So much about this business is an act of faith which is why I believe, even though the results are there for everyone to see, few trust it will continue and so do not become landlords.

HMOs have become an attractive thing to do in the property business. I find this very strange, as I have always said they have been the thing to do, but few seemed to believe me. When I began, whether you need planning to start a HMO was a grey area – no one was absolutely sure what the position was. Housing Standards hardly existed, and if you let to students you were generally considered exempt from the standards imposed by Housing Standards, as they were not considered to be HMOs. Then came the 2004 Housing Act with the introduction of licensing for three-storey or more HMOs. The Housing Act is an appalling, badly-drafted piece of legislation. One might only conclude that the parliamentary draftsmen were totally incompetent, which I do not believe. The government recruit the brightest lawyers, so you can only conclude that the government wanted to appear to do something but in reality, do very little with housing. It was a stab in the dark into an area which they have very little understanding of. Unfortunately, some councils took the new legislation as a green light to ramp up action against 'rogue landlords', a term I have difficulty understanding. If it means bad housing, then the biggest offenders are the councils themselves with their awful housing and practices. If you have any doubts, have a look at what are commonly referred to as 'sink estates'. If they mean evicting tenants without due process, then councils in their hostels and temporary housing are exempt and can and do evict at will, yet the very same council can get very precious about a private landlord doing the same. I am not suggesting we ignore bad landlords (whatever that means) but why do tenants use them? Why don't they move? In my area, there seems to be no shortage of housing; I always have voids. In areas where there is a shortage it may be another matter.

If we consider where HMOs and social housing collide, mostly in the area of letting to the unemployed, it again makes little sense. It is generally not known that Social Housing gets paid as much as ten times what the private sector is paid to house HMO tenants, sometimes more. Without many of the constraints the private sector has, Social Housing can evict at will; Social Housing does not have to follow any court procedure and is generally exempt from space standards. That is how many people can live in a particular size room, and it is not unheard of to allow a whole family to live in a room of 150 sq. ft., sharing a kitchen and bathroom.

The Rugg report of 2005 stated that in the private sector there is a paucity of research. We do not know how the housing market is working. The report is based on anecdotal evidence and often skewed towards London, and it appears this is all the press is concerned about. The London market has no connection as far as I can ascertain with, say, the Wolverhampton market. We continue to hear that because of average house prices, first time buyers cannot get on the housing ladder, and that buy-to-let investors are pricing first time buyers out of the market. It is all too general to be of much practical use. Should you invest in HMOs? The outlook is the same as when I first started in 1991 – impenetrable! The only current empirical evidence I can find is in the back of *Your Property Network*, a magazine for property investors, where the average rents for rooms are displayed. I would only take notice of areas where rents are increasing; reducing rents would be a no-no for me.

It is in times of uncertainty that the brave and foolish can make a fortune or a loss. The evidence of continual housing price rises is indisputable; the statistics are there, so if your HMO does not work hopefully property prices will have risen to bail you out. What do you have to lose?

I hope this short book will help you in your journey. Please do remember I am here to help you – see 'I want to hear from you' on page 17.

Best of luck,

Jim Haliburton
September 2017

PREFACE

I am often asked about or even criticised for including in books, articles or chapters, material that appears in my other books, or that has been published for free on my website or in other publications etc. I am also criticised for referring to my other publications or courses. I make no apology – if you don't like it please request your money back. I offer a no quibble 100% money back guarantee, less postage and packaging.

In property, common sense does not always apply. Some people like to pay for the convenience of having the best or most appropriate articles selected for them. I find it amazing what people will pay for, for example, water. The Consumer Association has pointed out that tap water is often better than bottled water, yet people still buy bottled water. One of these days, if the property market becomes unprofitable, I will consider selling fresh air. Yes, fresh air is free and all around us but I am confident that people will buy canned and compressed 'sea air', 'country air', 'morning dew air', 'Scottish loch mist' and so on. Then there is the sports angle with 'extra oxygen air' or 'ozone-improved air'. If any of my readers thinks the selling of fresh air is a good idea they are welcome to it, and I will be very grateful if you decide to pay me royalties for the idea, but to market fresh air, unlike property, you are going to need hundreds of thousands of pounds to start with and a massive marketing boost.

With property, if you follow my techniques you can get property for free and often only need to stick a card in the window to get tenants. Sorry – no comparison in my opinion to running any other business!

I WANT TO HEAR FROM YOU

As a reader of 'A Compendium of HMO Daddy's Blogs', you are its most important critic and commentator. I value your opinion and comments and want to know what else you would like me to include, as well as what you disagree with and any other words of wisdom you wish to offer.

You can email or write to me to let me know what you did or did not like, as well as what I can do to make it better, or what other information or service I could provide. Please note that I am often difficult to contact by phone because, as you can appreciate, I am very busy. But when I get a few spare minutes I love to talk about the business, so please do not be offended if I ask you to call back or leave a message.

If you are interested in finding out more, I also provide training courses on all aspects of my business, which you can find on my website www.hmodaddy.com.

When you write to me please include your name, email address, home address or phone number. I assure you I will value and review your comments.

Email: jim@hmodaddy.com

Website: www.hmodaddy.com

Mail: Jim Haliburton
            14 Walsall Road
            Wednesbury
            WS10 9JL

CHAPTER 1
WHAT TIPS CAN YOU GIVE A
NEW INVESTOR INTO HMOs?

MY TWELVE TOP TIPS FOR NEWBIE INVESTORS

1. Find a strategy and go with it

Investors now have it so much easier than when I started, as there is a lot more advice and financing available. I had very little help back in 1991 and financing was very limited, but the downside today is there is too much information and the newbie can suffer from information overload and 'analysis paralysis'. The ability to get financing is now much easier, provided you know where to look and are prepared to accept risk and be flexible and creative. I will obviously say HMOs are the best property strategy; I have looked and cannot find anything better. Get your strategy and get on with it. Just one HMO and less than ten years is often enough to make you self-sufficient – just imagine what five HMOs would do!

2. Act quickly

Good deals do not wait and if you delay you will lose them. You should be ready to take advantage of opportunities as they arise, so you need to know what you want and go for it. Do not let solicitors get in the way of making a deal.

3. Don't wait for the ideal deal

Make do with what is available. All properties improve with age in capital value and the income generated from rent usually increases, but you need to be patient outside the south east of England. It can take up to ten years to see any movement, but when property prices move they usually move without warning and do so rapidly. Assessing what rent to charge is much more difficult. A very rough guide is in the back of *Your Property Network*, a magazine for property investors which gives a survey of average rents. You can get a free copy of 'Your Property Network' at www.hmodaddy.com.

4. Hold, do not sell

Though HMOs are profitable, the capital appreciation is usually a lot more awesome, so it pays to hold. The first few properties I bought in the 90s and turned into HMOs are now worth as much as ten times what I paid. If you need cash, re-mortgage. Since HMOs have good income, you are usually able to cash out, i.e. release money by re-mortgaging. And a cash out is tax-free!

5. Learn, learn, learn

You never know it all – well actually I might, as I rarely hear anything I don't already know. Attending courses or reading, listening to and watching training material reminds and inspires me to improve, especially if I see what others are doing with property. A word of caution: don't believe everything you hear, but don't dismiss the implausible. I will let you into a secret: property is difficult and frightening. Many landlords are struggling and it is not an easy business. Some just don't realise it, are unaffected by it or just very good at concealing their struggles.

6. Keep it local

You are running a business, so it is very difficult, but not impossible to manage if your customers are miles away.

No one else will look after your business better than you. Keep hands on.

7. Be a landlord

I find tenants fascinating; they never cease to amaze me in so many ways. Take no notice of all this passive income nonsense, it is just a way to give a large slice of your profit (if not all) to someone else, who will usually do a much poorer job than you can and charge an extortionate amount for doing so.

8. You are on your own

If you don't expect anyone else to fight your corner, you will not be disappointed. Though I have never come across a landlord who is not prepared to give advice, albeit reluctantly, when asked. I often wonder if many landlords understand what they are doing, so I don't always believe it or follow their advice. You are very much on your own here and have to learn to make your own decisions, which includes deciding whether to take advice from so-called 'professionals'. I find these people often have their own agenda, which involves covering their own liability and maximising their own profit. Helping you rarely comes into their equation. I have often ignored advice from professionals and been far better off doing so, and the opposite has happened: I have in fact been worse off by following their advice. Things keep changing, so you cannot always expect to travel down the same road as others and get the same results. Many of the most awesome deals I have made were known to others but were ignored, as they could not see the potential or were afraid of the risk.

9. Avoid officialdom

Officials are rarely of any help; they will often demand you do things that neither you nor your tenants want nor need. They are not landlords and do not appreciate or care about your problems or the enormous costs they impose upon you. View them as a tax on doing business. Apart from a few basic safety requirements like fitting smoke detectors (the number of detectors you need is a matter of opinion) and gas and electricity safety checks, which amongst many other things are legal requirements so must be done, despite their questionable value. The rest is of little benefit. Many of these officials are anti-private landlord or against the development of housing. I should love them because they deter landlords and are the cause of our housing shortage, which is why there is a demand for HMOs. However, I would suggest for your own business success and sanity that you avoid them, and learn how to handle them should they catch up with you.

10. Don't trust professionals

Ask yourself – what are they getting out of this? They will often give advice which is not in your own best interest, but which reduces their liability and will rack up their fees. The exception is solicitors when it comes to litigation, which they like to avoid with good reason. You, on the other hand, need to make your own decision about whether or not to sue.

11. Don't expect perfection

No one is perfect – work with people to get the best you can out of them. This includes yourself; it is all about making the best of what you have. The art lies in knowing when enough is enough and moving on, or deciding that the incompetence you put up with is better than nothing. Don't believe what you often hear from other landlords that they have perfect staff, builders, tenants. They are either delusional, or, more likely disingenuous – that is, assuming they even have staff, builders, or tenants.

12. Remember your goal

When it all feels like too much – and it will – remember, in the long term if you stick at it you will be wealthy beyond your dreams and the arsehole who is upsetting you will still be an arsehole and no doubt still broke.

CHAPTER 2
WHAT COSTLY MISTAKES CAN
AN HMO INVESTOR MAKE?

FIFTEEN COSTLY MISTAKES AN INVESTOR
CAN MAKE USING THE HMO STRATEGY

Introduction: I have listed the mistakes in what I deem to be their cost-order. For more on making and saving money from HMOs, see my book *35 Money Making or Saving Tips for HMO Landlords*, available from my website www.hmodaddy.com. Using only five tips from my *35 Money Making or Saving Tips for HMO Landlords* could increase your net income from your HMOs by 20%, which means that for every five HMOs you have you will have the profit of six. Imagine what you could do with the extra money!

Be kind to yourself when it comes to making mistakes. Mistakes are part of the learning process and I am sure you have heard the saying: 'The person who doesn't make a mistake is the person who never did anything'. I would add that they have in fact made the biggest mistake by doing nothing with their lives.

1. **The biggest and most costly mistake** an investor can make is not to invest in HMOs or to delay doing so. This dwarfs the 14 other costly mistakes I have listed – they are but a speck in comparison. You could say all the rest do not matter in comparison. Property prices have in many areas gone up faster than an average wage earner can afford. Just owning a house could have over the last 40 years made more money just on the capital appreciation than could be earned by working for the same period, never mind the income that could have been achieved by multi-letting it.

2. **Professionals can be part of the problem:** Ask yourself – what are they getting out of this? They will often give advice which will rack up their fees or reduce their liability, not what is in your best interest. They are, with good reason, cautious and very anti-litigation. You on the other hand need to make your own decisions. In retrospect I have lost a fortune by following their advice by not buying when I should have.

3. **Do the numbers:** An HMO is rarely profitable with fewer than 5 tenants. The more rooms, the more profit. In my experience the running costs are not proportional. In other words, it costs the same to run a 4-bed HMO as it does an 8-bed. Alternatively, an 8-bed HMO costs no more to run than a 4-bed. The fifth tenant is usually the profit, which means that if you have fewer than four tenants you are losing money. Another way of looking at this is that a 6-bed HMO makes the same profit as having two 5-bed HMOs. The mind boggles at the profit from a 9-bed HMO – the same as five or more 5-bed HMOs! The running costs are greater once you get over around 8-beds, but I still find that larger HMOs are phenomenally profitable and not much more difficult to manage.

4. **Be a landlord:** Do not expect others to run your properties for you. Rarely will others run your business as well as you can and will charge a lot of money for not very good service. Worse, they will sometimes make it very much harder than operating the business yourself.

5. **Avoid staff:** Unless you know how to handle staff, keep well away. Very few people have experience selecting, motivating and managing staff, yet nearly everyone thinks they are an expert because they have worked for an employer. I can assure you it is not the same thing. Be very careful when considering taking on staff, and here

is the rub – you will often need to take on staff if you wish to expand. Nothing I know can prepare you for employing people – even those who have employed others are not much help. They say the same: they will never employ anyone again.

6. **Do not mix types and ages:** Keep types and ages of tenants the same, i.e. all workers or professionals or DSS, and in the same age group. For example, do not mix a house of middle-aged professionals with unemployed or younger professionals as it will usually upset the existing tenants and they may leave.

7. **Let with care:** Be cautious when letting as mistakes can be very costly. Not only might you not get paid, but you could lose all your other tenants and have the property damaged. The saying that an empty room is the cheapest option is very often true.

8. **Evict a bad tenant quickly:** Know the legal process and implications. In my experience a bad tenant, whether antisocial or a rent defaulter, becomes worse. Start the eviction process immediately after the tenant defaults or begins to become a problem. For more on how to evict, see my manual *DIY Eviction* which explains the correct process, and if you want to learn the awful consequences

of getting the eviction process wrong, please read my book *HMOs and Compensation for Unlawful Eviction*, both available from www.hmodaddy.com.

9. **Avoid the unemployed:** That is, unless you know how to manage this market. I should add it is the minority of tenants who cause problems, but when they do those problems can be enormous, leading to the closure of and sometimes massive damage to the HMO. The tenants' behaviour is the main problem and the Housing Benefit system is a nightmare to deal with until you know how to work it. For more, see my book *An Introduction to Letting to the Unemployed for HMO Landlords*, available from www.hmodaddy.com.

10. **Limit gas, electricity and water usage:** You need to introduce ways to restrict or limit the cost of utilities, especially when housing the unemployed. Workers and professionals tend to be more responsible and do not abuse the utilities so often. I have discussed the various ways you can restrict or limit the use of utilities in my manual *How to Become a Multi-Millionaire HMO Landlord*, available from www.hmodaddy.com.

11. **Failure to comply with standards:** Whichever standards your council seeks to impose, it is usually best to comply. Do not ignore officials as they can be very

nasty and you could end up with a closure order and/or thousands of pounds in fines. Additionally you must be prepared to stand your ground if officials are wrong, which surprisingly more often than you would think. Enforcement is quite variable and most of what can be demanded is not needed, nor is of benefit to or wanted by tenants. Find out what your council demands from you and comply within limits. You should always, at the very basic, have some fire detectors. Also, know the procedures to object to, as often they are very time limited, and by being out of time you will have things imposed which, if you had appealed against them in time would have probably gone away. For more on standards and what your council can and cannot make you do, get my manual *How to Become a Multi-Millionaire HMO Landlord*, available from www.hmodaddy.com.

12. **Don't give too much**: Tenants want a room and expect to pay for everything else. Giving tenants extra is often more about the landlord's ego than what the tenant wants or will pay for. What attracts a tenant and what they will pay for is what matters. The tenant will take whatever you give, then turn it around and blame you when it does not work. The saying that 'No good deed goes unpunished' is very true in relation to this business. I now give tenants the very basic and charge for everything else so if they are not happy with what I supply it gives them less justification to withhold rent.

13. **Avoid officialdom:** They are rarely any help and will often demand you do things that neither you nor your tenants want or need. They are not landlords and do not appreciate or care about your problems or the enormous costs they impose upon you. Look upon them as a tax on doing business. Apart from a few basic safety requirements like fire detectors and gas and electricity safety, amongst many other things which are legal requirements (though much of this is of questionable value), the rest is of little benefit. Many of these officials are anti-private landlord or against the development of housing. I should love them because they deter landlords and are the cause of our housing shortage, which is why there is a demand for HMOs. However, I would suggest, for your own business success and sanity, that you avoid and learn how to handle them should they catch up with you.

14. **Be flexible but don't show it**: Something is better than nothing – an empty room brings in no rent, but giving a rent reduction to some and not others causes problems. You will get dissatisfied tenants if you charge them differently without good reason, as tenants talk to each other and tell other tenants what they pay. However, to make a profit you will need to fill and keep your properties at capacity so occasionally being flexible will help.

15. **Undercharging rent**: You are running a business: the rent is set by the market regardless of cost. I know this seems counter-intuitive, but I have yet to find much evidence that charging a low rent attracts or keeps tenants. Being flexible on terms can make a difference, but flexibility has its problems (see 14 above), and probably only makes a marginal difference to being able to let the room, though this may only apply to my area. In other parts of the country the rent charged may be critical. If you are making a good profit, save it in a reserve fund for when the market turns and you are not making a profit.

CHAPTER 3
HOW DID I BECOME A SUCCESSFUL INVESTOR?

For a start, I do not think that I am very successful – I could have done an awful lot better! I have made some horrendous mistakes. I've wasted so much opportunity that I could have bought and run a luxury yacht on the lost proceeds.

Some think I am successful because I have so many properties and tenants, but business is all about maximising profit and minimising work. I am self-indulgent and do far, far too much because I like to. Rather than treating it as a business, I see it as a game I enjoy. I should be ruthlessly focused on increasing profit, decreasing costs and doing a lot less work. I work obscenely long hours which I struggle to control. Even on the occasional holiday I still work because I enjoy it.

I sometimes wonder what would have happened if I had only kept to the first five properties I purchased in the 90s and not acquired any more. Those initial five properties are now worth about ten times what I paid for them, are nearly always full and would probably net me, if self-managed, well over £100k pa. I estimate that I could manage those five properties in less than three hours per week, providing I employed others to clean, redecorate and undertake major repairs. I cannot imagine what I would be doing now if I was in that situation as I often spend more time than that 'working' before even going into the office.

I think I can sum it all up with the phrase I 'Just do it', though I feel I could have done much, much better in retrospect, especially if I had started earlier and bought more. As I said, initially I was very cautious and the few early purchases are now worth ten times or more than what I paid for them. Rents have also doubled since I started which is nowhere near the capital appreciation the same properties have made. It is probably the realisation that if I had bought earlier, I would have been in a much better position now, that helped spur my later acquisitions.

I can think of no other business where the cost of the working assets remains fixed yet the value of the assets increases along with the income. Unfortunately, I have only acquired most of my properties in the last ten years, before the recession. Though profitable, they have seen nothing like the appreciation of my earlier purchases and little increase in rental income. This business usually requires about ten or twenty years between purchase and success, and enormous tenacity to stick at it through the ups and downs. I hope I never become like so many that take the quick way out and sell up for a good profit when they first hit a problem.

CHAPTER 4
WHAT MAKES YOU DIFFERENT FROM ORDINARY INVESTORS?

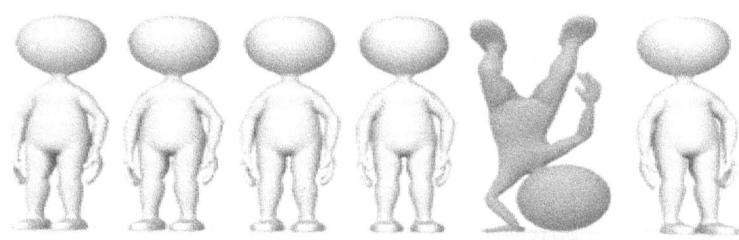

What makes me different? I am not sure; I have not done very much analysis on what others are doing. However, from a casual observation I can ascertain that:

1. **I do it** – a lot do nothing or very little. I do not wait for the perfect deal to come along but make do with what property is available and that I can cashflow. Cashflow means after getting all the purchase costs back by borrowing and covering all expenses, the property still makes money. Nor do I spend much time with the 'why' or 'what' – I just get on with buying property. There is no master or exit plan!

2. **I am not cautious** – I have what even I say is a breathtaking faith that property will work out well. Generally, if I can, I will acquire a property that is viable and will rarely refuse a property on which I can make a profit.

3. **I don't seek out BMV deals** – it is what I can make on or out of the deal that matters. If it makes a good profit it does not matter what it costs, but obviously I try and buy at the best price possible. (BMV: below market price. The property is purchased at a discount.)

4. **I keep to the HMO strategy** – I have adapted to take all types of tenants to fill my available units, though I generally prefer working and professional tenants and am not so keen on most of the unemployed. I am not so sure that keeping to only one property strategy (i.e. HMOs) is ideal, but I have tried other strategies and they have not worked anywhere near as well. Maybe I should be more persistent.

5. **I am not deterred by officials** – I generally know what I can and cannot do and do not rely on the Council's often creative interpretation of what I am allowed to or more often not allowed to do.

6. **Involvement** – unlike most landlords, I feel it is my duty to involve myself in landlord associations and local authority groups, through which I have devoted a considerable amount of time to try to improve the landlord's lot.

7. **Help for other landlords** – I have attempted to help other landlords and newbie investors. As a result, I have produced two books: *101 Questions and Answers for HMO Landlords* and *Top Twelve Current Issues for HMO Landlords*. I am now well into a third book, *More 101 Questions and Answers for HMO Landlords*. These books are available from www.hmodaddy.com. I am the only landlord I know who holds himself out to provide anyone who wishes to learn the business with free work experience. See HMO Academy on www.hmodaddy.com for details, which provides an extensive range of information for HMO landlords.

8. **I believe in what I do** – providing accommodation may not rank alongside ending world hunger, but I do what I do with passion. I provide the highest quality accommodation of its type in my area and have no eviction policy for those who cannot afford to pay rent, though I rarely find anyone who cannot pay, just those who refuse to pay. If I have suitable accommodation I will not turn any genuine applicant away just because

they do not have any money. I am the only private landlord I know who provides a tenants' charter.

9. **I like tenants** – it annoys me to hear this nonsense about providing a hands-off or passive investment. To use others to manage your property is a bit like being a footballer but not playing football or owning a fantastic swimming pool and not using it. I find dealing with tenants to be very satisfying.

10. **Care for tenants** – like many landlords I care about my tenants. I have never evicted a tenant who could not pay, only those who deliberately refuse to pay. I even house those who are genuinely homeless but have no money, rather than letting them sleep on the streets. The standard of my accommodation is better than that of most of my competitors. I provided a tenants' charter and eviction protocol long before the social sector was forced to do so, and it is better in standards.

CHAPTER 5
WHAT SUCCESS STORIES DO YOU HAVE?

I tend to be cautious about speaking about my successes. It is probably a lot to do with my childhood, which taught me to keep very quiet about what I wanted – as this is what those who ran the children's home that I was brought up in, would take away from me as a punishment for things which even now I cannot fathom I had done. I, therefore, don't like to say much about what is going well, but this is a story which has such enormous learning potential attached to it that I feel I must tell it if only to help others.

I am often asked how I get deals, and I sense that the audience disengages at the answer for two reasons. First, people assume I get the deals because I am who I am. It is easy for me but impossible for them. Second, getting deals is very easy and people don't, for some reason, want to believe this and try to over-complicate it in search of a magic formula. For more on this, read *How do I get deals?* available from www.hmodaddy.com.

I was asked this very question at the end of a recent course and I proceeded to answer the question to what was, as usual, an incredulous audience who just would not believe that deals were there for the taking. I was explaining how easy it was to get property: it is all around you, you just must be aware of the possibilities. It is so much easier for newbies now than when I started, with all the relaxation in planning and the wealth of financing now available. I mentioned that you can turn offices into residential use flats and houses without planning permission, which triggered one in the audience, a surveyor – I will call him 'Bob' – to say he had an office block which he had been trying to get rid of for a client for three years without luck. I used this office block as an illustration of just how easy it was to get property, so Bob and I discussed its potential.

The office was right in the centre of Coventry, a ten minute walk from the University and mainline train station, which was only fifty minutes from London Euston. Coventry is considered one of the top spots for accommodation in the UK. Bob went on to explain that he had been approached by a purchaser who had discussed the idea of turning the office block into an HMO, but he had dismissed the idea as fantasy.

Now I had mentioned it he realised the buyer may have had a point. I asked if anyone was interested in his office block – no reply.

I explained that office blocks were easy to convert into HMOs and asked what the difference was between an office and an HMO room. Answer: add a bed. With students you don't even have to remove the office desk or chair. Most offices have kitchens and bathrooms. Ok, they could do with being made more residential, e.g. curtains instead of blinds etc., but not that much necessarily needs changing.

To encourage interest in the office block, I went on to say that I would visit it with anyone who was interested in the deal to help them assess its potential. Here was a leasehold property which Bob, after a bit of encouragement, was saying the owners would be prepared to even give a year's rent-free period for; it was potentially a free property.

I even went on to say that because they had been a great audience, I would give to anyone in the room free assistance to assess the office block and show them how to finance it and make it truly a 'no money deal'. Still no reaction! I said I had a team to do the building work and contacts in the area who could manage the property. Still no reaction! I was frustrated: here was a property for nothing yet no one reacted or even showed interest! By the way, this behaviour is not unusual: people say they want to get into property, but when given the deal of the decade they don't proceed. I have seen it time and time again but never with a whole course. It is usually on an individual basis. I went on to answer a few more questions and the course finished and we then retired to the bar.

I had forgotten about the deal until Bob called me the next day. He thought I was seriously interested in the office block myself as I had enthusiastically kept on about it. I have rules in deciding what to invest in, and one is not to invest outside my area. This property was about an hour away. However, I agreed I would look at it to show Bob what he could do with it. After we had assessed the property, Bob decided he could not take it on, mainly because he felt it would amount to a conflict of interest since he worked for the owners. Luckily, I had been thinking of diversifying areas. I still bitterly regret not buying in London, but property there has always been too expensive compared to where I am. In hindsight though it was ridiculously cheap, actually a phenomenal bargain!

I eventually, with Bob's persuasion, decided to take on the office block and turn it into a 26-bed HMO property. Most people could retire just on this one deal.

Anyone on the course could have had this deal. I was prepared to assist them, but no one was interested. Success was only a decision away. All they had to do was say yes! It was a no money deal! I would walk them through the rest, as I have done so many times.

CHAPTER 6
HOW DO YOU AVOID HOUSING BENEFIT RECLAIMS?

Many landlords who house the unemployed have an issue with the Council recovering rent paid to them, known as reclaims. The Council's Housing

Benefit department has a duty to recover overpaid Local Housing Allowance (LHA) and prefers to recover it from the landlord or agent, usually by automatically deducting it from the rent payment. It is easier to recover from the landlord or agent than the tenant. Landlords and agents feel this is unfair, as they have housed the tenant and now have to repay the Council money paid to them as rent, often by the Council deducting it from rent payments for other tenants of the landlord or agent, sometimes years after the original tenant has left. As the tenant is unemployed, the landlord stands very little chance of recovering the money from the tenant. It is an unjust system and a slap in the face to landlords and agents who house some of the most challenging tenants. Dealing with the extra administration that LHA creates for the landlord is ignored and not paid for by the Council, who will say that LHA is the tenant's benefit and no concern of the landlord or agent, yet it is the landlord's problem when it comes to overpayment.

The standard advice to avoid a reclaim is not to house LHA tenants, or if you do, to not receive LHA payment yourself but have the tenants paid directly. In other words, the tenant receives the LHA payment, and because they are paid direct the rules say the Housing Benefit department cannot reclaim from the landlord. However, allowing direct payment to the tenant is not a sensible course of action for the following five reasons.

The five reasons a landlord should have payments made to themselves:

1. **A landlord will lose far more rent if the tenant receives the LHA directly, as the tenant is inclined to keep it. It is safer if the landlord receives direct payment and risks reclaims.**

The problem with this approach is that it is almost impossible in some areas for the landlord to get paid LHA directly to start with. The tenant usually has to be in arrears, and even then the landlord has to demand direct payment. Housing Benefit departments are supposed to allow, if requested, direct payment to the landlord if the tenant is vulnerable or unlikely to pay, but this is often very restrictively interpreted and rarely allowed, so in practice the tenant has to be in arrears before the landlord can receive direct payment. Often, just one missed payment is sufficient and the landlord can get direct payment on the grounds that the tenant is unlikely to pay. This may sound good in theory, but in practice the first payment is often a substantial sum of money usually averaging over 8 weeks' rent because of the time it takes for LHA to be assessed. Getting back to the point: why should a landlord try to receive direct payment?

Who should receive payment is an on-balance argument. It's a case of judging how many HMO tenants will pay their landlord if they get their rent paid to themselves, compared with how much will be reclaimed from the landlord if the landlord receives the money. If the tenant receives the money themselves my experience is that only 20% of my LHA tenants will pay. Appreciate that it is not a crime if a tenant keeps the rent. Housing Benefit will do nothing about unpaid rent apart from using it as grounds to pay the landlord directly, but only if the landlord asks for direct payment. They will not stop or reclaim the LHA from the tenant. Worse, Housing Benefit departments know this is going on and do not warn the landlord. You can begin to understand now why tenants keep the rent, as there are no consequences apart from possible eviction. What would you do in the situation if you were single and had no attachment to a particular property or landlord? Appreciate that the rent paid in most areas is often a lot more than the tenant receives to live on.

However, to argue the contrary, if the landlord sets up a 'ring-fenced' bank account for the tenant, the landlord is usually always paid, and in my experience it is a very safe way to be paid. The LHA is automatically paid direct to the landlord via the tenant's bank account. Odd as it may sound, this is classified as direct payment to the tenant as the money is paid into the tenant's bank account. The principle is that the tenant has set up this account, usually with the landlord's help, and that the tenant can cancel the bank account at any time without reference to the landlord.

I would argue that a landlord is better off receiving the LHA directly, as one can arrange payment directly to the tenant and still be paid – but I will develop this point in sections 2 to 5 below. I appreciate there is a very subtle difference between the landlord being paid directly via a ring-fenced bank account and being paid directly, but the law is often based on subtle distinctions. If it works, don't knock it. I use ring-fenced accounts for all our new tenants and then when they get into eight weeks arrears change to direct payment. However, initial indications are that under Universal Credit, the long-delayed system which is replacing LHA, using a ring-fenced bank account may not be as easy as it once was in guaranteeing payment to the landlord. We have yet to see how it will work.

Also in support of having direct payment to the landlord, I cannot recall having to repay rent that I am entitled to as I always challenge any repayment I disagree with (see 2 below). For instance, I do not object to a reclaim for rent after I have notified the Housing Benefit department that the tenant has left and they continue to pay me, as they so often do – nor do I thank them for their interest free loans, which perhaps I should!

The opposite can happen when tenants receive benefit direct to themselves. Any over-payment should be reclaimed from the tenant, even though the landlord has received benefit to which they are not entitled, for example if the tenant has left, in which case the tenant must reclaim the money from the landlord. A landlord could be receiving payment for quite some time for a tenant who has left, and just as with all other automatic payments, cannot reject them or stop receiving them. The tenant has to stop the payment, though the landlord is obliged to notify the Council if he knows the tenant is receiving LHA. I believe that landlords may be unjustly enriched by this twist, as some tenants are unlikely to chase their ex-landlord for the overpayment as they either just don't care or can't be bothered.

2. Most reclaims can be successfully challenged.

Many landlords do not realise that Housing Benefit departments – even though the landlord is receiving direct payment from the Council – are supposed to ascertain from whom it is fair to reclaim the rent. As a generalisation a landlord will only have to repay if:

i. **The tenant has passed away**. Thankfully, death is a fairly rare event and the risk of substantial overpayments can be reduced by carrying out regular checks on your tenants. It is a legal requirement that HMO landlords undertake regular checks of their HMOs. We also charge a 'top up', which is where we charge extra rent above the LHA rate and expect the tenant to pay. It is another way of checking if the tenant is still alive or in occupation (see below). I have never ever received a top up from a dead tenant or from a tenant who has left. Many landlords I suspect don't worry about this and treat any overpayment as an interest free loan even though they have to repay it.

ii. **The tenant has left**. The landlord is expected by the Housing Benefit system to keep a close check on the tenant to ensure they are in occupation, though the courts could look upon this as harassment. Harassment seems to cover anything the landlord does which upsets the tenant, including asking for rent.

In other words, a landlord rarely legally has to repay rent and only does so because they are either incompetent or frightened to challenge their Housing Benefit department. Don't be – they won't take it personally, and if they do you should not care. Sometimes you will have to go as far as appealing to the appeal tribunal. To cope with the Housing Benefit system, one needs to assert oneself. The system is riddled with incompetence and prejudice against landlords because they are perceived as unjustly making money. If you are to survive you have to be prepared to fight hard. Be totally relentless, know the system and don't be afraid to push hard for every penny to which you are entitled. From long experience I have no doubt that there are many who work in the Housing Benefit department who take great pleasure in ensuring landlords do not get paid and will do their utmost to screw up claims. When I complain to their bosses, I have had the reply that the member of staff who I am complaining about 'does not work for us anymore'. The senior officers, in my experience, generally want to do a decent job and are surprisingly approachable and act on complaints, so it pays to go to the top whenever necessary.

One of the many problems an LHA landlord has with Housing Benefit departments is that they tend to believe everything the tenant says about the landlord and disbelieve anything the landlord says that increases their income or prevents their Housing Benefit income being reduced. They rarely disbelieve a landlord when he says something which saves the Housing Benefit department money, such as when the tenant has left, but do not believe the landlord if he says the tenant is still in occupation.

I have managed to challenge reclaims where the tenants have alleged that they have left, but it is very difficult to prove the tenant has not left or that the reclaim should come from the tenant. I have known tenants to claim at two addresses for reasons I can only speculate at. Also appreciate that Housing Benefit departments rarely take notice of any contractual requirement of the tenant to give any notice of leaving. The other odd thing is that Housing Benefit will use the fact that the tenant is claiming elsewhere as evidence that they have left your property, but never that the tenant is not claiming. Where do the Housing Benefit department think the tenant must be living if they are not living at my property or claiming elsewhere?

An example of a successful reclaim:

I had left a note on the back of an old envelope asking the tenant when was he going to pay his top up (the difference paid by the Housing Benefit and the rent) and he replied on the envelope, saying he was leaving at the end of the week. The envelope had been franked with a date and I produced the old envelope to show that the tenant was still at the premises after that date and he admitted he was still in occupation, albeit only to the end of the week. The tenant had, it turned out, told the Housing Benefit department he had left a few months earlier than the date on the envelope, and had been claiming Housing Benefit for another property but still using my property. He did not tell me he had left, only that he was going to leave, and it was not obvious from my regular checks that he had left. I was extremely lucky that I had kept the old envelope the tenant had written on, as I very much doubt the Housing Benefit department would have believed me.

If the tenant starts work or has a change in circumstances the landlord is not generally expected to know and as such can usually successfully challenge a reclaim. We have always been successful in this respect.

It is not generally appreciated by landlords that by law, if the tenant is not physically staying at the property they are claiming for but living at another property, whether claiming or not at the other property, or if they are sleeping on the street or on a friend's or relative's sofa, they are not entitled to the LHA for the property they have claimed for and it can be reclaimed by the Housing Benefit department. I know this is nonsense and it is impractical and unlawful for landlords to make bed checks, however I do not make the law and it is one of the many problems you face when housing LHA tenants.

The position is even more complex than this: periods of non-occupation due to the tenant being on holiday (yes, LHA tenants can have holidays), in hospital or in prison for short periods still count as being in occupation, yet the landlord has difficulty in knowing that the tenant is on holiday, in hospital or in prison – and if in prison, the length of the sentence. To add to this, if the landlord makes a mistake in treating the tenant as abandoned then they risk being sued for substantial compensation for unlawful eviction – see my book HMOs and Compensation for Unlawful Eviction available from www.hmodaddy.com. It is a truly horrifying read and shows the bias against landlords from the judicial system.

My golden tip – challenge every unfair reclaim. We always do, when we believe the decision is wrong. When challenged, the Housing Benefit department usually says it has made a mistake and refunds the deduction. Would I be cynical if I were to say there was a policy of automatically reclaiming from the landlord by Housing Benefit departments, which has a lot to do with them getting a 50% bonus from the government for every pound they reclaim? Many landlords believe that their Housing Benefit departments act with integrity and within the law and must be correct when making a reclaim. My experience, as illustrated above, clearly shows the contrary.

I estimate that millions of pounds have been wrongly reclaimed by Housing Benefit departments automatically reclaiming from the landlord. More fool landlords for not challenging reclaims. I also wonder if the departments are doing the same to tenants.

3. **Even having payments made directly to the tenant does not stop Housing Benefit departments from trying to reclaim payments.**

I admit it is extremely rare for this to happen but we have had two such instances, both of which involving substantial sums of money and of unique circumstances. We successfully appealed against both reclaims but had to take them to a tribunal hearing.

I will give the facts of one of the cases: a homeless tenant with an alcohol problem was placed with us by the very council who then reclaimed nearly all the rent they had paid us, which was about 12 months' worth, even though it was we who notified them that the tenant had abandoned. Abandonment is the normal way such tenants leave. They rarely notify you that they are going to leave or have left, and often leave behind many possessions. The council said when they placed the tenant with us that they would provide support for the tenant as he was classified as vulnerable. We have since discovered this rarely happens once they have duped you into providing the tenant with accommodation.

When we investigated the reclaim, the Housing Benefit department alleged that they had phoned the tenant on his mobile phone after we said he had left and asked him when he had left, and he had replied, 'About a year ago'.

Without any another contact or investigation this was sufficient for the Housing Benefit department to reclaim 12 months' rent, i.e. for most of the period the tenant had been living in the bedsit, without any reference to us, that is, on the say-so of a raging alcoholic with a history of homelessness who had been placed with us by their own housing support team who were supposed to be supporting the tenant and were no doubt being paid a substantial amount of money to do so. For a start, we found the fact that the Housing Benefit department had been able to talk to the tenant on his mobile very odd, as this type of tenant rarely keeps the same mobile number for more than a few weeks, never mind for a year. We had also, in attempting to see if he had abandoned and was not, say, in hospital, tried to call the tenant and his next of kin without success. When we let we always ask for and check the tenant's mobile phone number by calling them, and we ask for next of kin. Also, up until he abandoned, our regular weekly checks of the property had shown no indication the tenant was not in occupation.

The rent was being paid automatically from the tenant's bank account into ours and continued to be paid until we notified the Housing Benefit department that the tenant had abandoned the property. The injustice of the situation was also rankled by the fact that no credit was given to us for our honesty in notifying the Housing Benefit department that the tenant was no longer in occupation. I felt that because we were housing a vulnerable tenant without the support the Council had promised, we should have been given some consideration, especially realising that if the tenant had been housed by the Council in supported accommodation it would have cost the taxpayer over ten times what we received. It was not as if the Housing Benefit department had discovered the tenant had left – we had brought it to their attention. The evidence later disclosed at the tribunal did not say that the tenant had been claiming LHA at another address, and it would have if the tenant had been claiming. Many landlords, I am sure, would have kept quiet about the tenant not being in occupation or may not have known the LHA can only be paid if the tenant is in regular occupation.

Returning to the alcoholic tenant: luckily the tribunal chairman quickly ascertained that the tenant was being paid directly, and therefore decided that the Housing Benefit department should reclaim the over-payment from the tenant, but not before he established that we had grounds to believe the tenant was still in occupation, which really should not have been relevant.

We had nearly five thousand pounds in rent refunded, though it took over six months from the decision to be repaid. The reason the Housing Benefit department gave for the delay was that they were considering appealing! For six months? As a result, because of the time it took to hear the case and get repaid, we had for well over a year been without this tenant's rent. I wonder how a Housing Benefit department officer would feel about having to wait for over twelve months to get paid a year's salary. Just what will happen if the tenant reclaims Housing Benefit? Will the Council try and reclaim the year's rent from the tenant? That would mean the reclaim will be deducted from his rent next time he claims, so the next landlord will not receive the full rent.

4. It costs nothing to receive direct payment.

This is my main argument for payment being sent straight to the landlord. The payment services, i.e. the 'ring-fenced bank accounts' that LHA tenants can use, usually deduct a large handling charge. The accounts which will receive LHA for the tenant and then pay the landlord charge between 50p and £12 per payment (yes, as much as £12 per payment!), with the average around £4 per payment. This is deducted from the rent (benefit) we receive, and tenants are reluctant to pay this charge, arguing that they only opened the account because we insisted they must. We would not have housed them had they refused to open the account. There is also a move made by some of these so-called 'banks' to make the landlord pay their high charges as a condition of letting the tenant use their service.

I estimate that we are much better off receiving direct payment and risking the occasional reclaim than we would be to pay a third party to pay us the LHA the tenant receives. The very rare occasion the tenant stops payment to their 'ring-fenced' bank account and keeps the payment adds weight to this point. Unfortunately, many of these payment services are politically motivated towards tenants and so are disinclined to co-operate with the landlord when a tenant does this without notifying their landlord.

You need to be very vigilant in checking that payments received are correct, which is difficult to do if you receive multiple payments from the same 'bank', as they sometimes do not identify payments. You receive just one payment for all of your tenants, and by a process of elimination, or, if your housing benefit department co-operates with you and tells you who has changed who they pay to, you can find out who is not paying. Such a process can take a lot of effort.

5. Universal Credit will continue direct payment to landlords.

We do not know how Universal Credit (the new way Housing Benefit will be paid) is going to be implemented, but it is being said that direct payments to landlords with the new system will remain how they have already been set up. Whether this will happen we have yet to find out. The position is even more unclear about the 'ring-fenced' bank accounts. I have no doubt that many tenants will take advantage of any change to keep the rent money for their personal use.

Conclusion

I would always get direct payment to myself as landlord if I can, as it is a far more certain and cheaper way of receiving benefit. Remember my golden tip: always challenge a reclaim if you have grounds and you will not have to repay rent unreasonably. There are also rumours that Universal Credit, the system that is replacing LHA, will honour direct payment to landlords when the tenant moves from LHA to Universal Credit. For more on handling LHA tenants get my manual *An HMO Landlord's Guide to Letting to The Unemployed* available exclusively from my website www.hmodaddy.com.

CHAPTER 7
WHAT UNUSUAL PROPERTIES
HAVE YOU ACQUIRED?

I don't consider a property unusual when I buy it, but may do so upon reflection when others question my purchases. It is only then that I appreciate that what I have bought may seem an unusual or strange choice.

We all make assumptions as to what is normal and about how other people should live. Many assume that everyone wants to live like them and provide HMOs accordingly. On the other hand, if you listen to old people reminiscing with affection about living in overcrowded properties with very basic amenities, you will question how important property condition is.

The most unusual purchase I think I ever made was a derelict Grade 2 listed building. Initially, I considered it a beautiful, fantastic building, and it was cheap. I was not expecting the opposition I experienced from the Council, who previously owned the building. I went on to receive and appreciate the enormous cost and complexity in repairing such a building. My initial enquiries to the Conservation Department informed me that they were not concerned with what I did with the building so long as I did not change the outside and that no, they didn't provide any grants to assist in the cost of the renovation, nor did they have the manpower to come and give any help or advice, 'Sonny'.

Yes, they referred to me as 'Sonny'. The clear message I received was that they were far too busy to be bothered with the building and that the listing only affected the exterior.

So, along with reassurance from my builder that it would not cost much to restore, I bought the building. Relying on this information was a mistake: the Conservation Department later, following a complaint, decided to take an interest in the building and denied giving the information that they were only concerned with the exterior. However, they could not decide what they wanted me to do with the building, yet felt free to criticise me for the extensive damage they, the

Council, had caused to the building whilst under their ownership. The indecision of the Council assisted the builders in racking up enormous costs, but at a fraction of what it cost the Council to renovate similar buildings. So, after much delay, I cracked on and finished renovating it to let it as a HMO.

The Council could not afford to repair or maintain listed buildings in their ownership and had themselves done a lot of damage, or should I say desecrated the building, by means of bodged repairs and ripping out many of its features, including the windows and doors. On top of that, the unnecessary costs they were trying to impose did not seem to matter very much to them. It was as though there were rules for me, a private landlord, but none for themselves.

If this was not bad enough, the building was in the middle of nowhere, about a mile from the nearest bus stop and in a graveyard which the Council locked up at 5pm, restricting access to a hole in the fence. What chance had I of letting it? Oddly, as it turned out the HMO lets reasonably well, which opens an interesting debate as to where to buy an HMO!

I do not think I will be able to top this as the most unusual property deal I have made. I have better stories from other landlords which are included in my book *HMO Daddy Reveals All*, available from my website www.hmodaddy.com.

CHAPTER 8
WHAT DO YOU MOST ENJOY ABOUT PROPERTY?

enjoy!

I wonder why people who are paying good money to learn from me about property ask me this question. What does it matter to them? They will also often say that I don't seem to be very happy with what I am doing. The important thing is yourself: my motivation and enjoyment are unlikely to be the same as yours.

However, for those who are curious, I will try to explain what I do, but I don't like to delve too much into what I think. A psychologist will say our motivation has a lot to do with our childhood, and you will excuse me if I don't want to return to being a lonely, unloved and brutalised child in a children's home, or re-experience the guilt in knowing I don't feel grateful to those who run such places, or remember that I should get over it as I have survived while others suffered and continue to suffer far worse. So my explanation may not be as accurate as demanded in other areas of my business. The fact is, I do enjoy the property business and cannot stop doing property-related things.

What I probably enjoy most about property is talking and writing about it, helping other investors with their issues and running courses. See my website, www.hmodaddy.com, for more details of books I have written and courses and services I offer.

Owning the number of properties I do demands a team of staff. I gain tremendous satisfaction in sorting out problems, but doing so can be overwhelming. Whatever I concentrate on takes all my time and effort. If I focus on gardening, I can spend all my time dealing with gardens, if it is rent collecting then this absorbs all my time and it is never finished. Meanwhile, more gardens need doing and more tenants need chasing for rent or evicting. I have to flit between all aspects of my business, and the satisfaction of seeing a job well done or completed is gone. I have the frustration of trying to get others to undertake the jobs that I could complete to a higher standard, and often more quickly if I had the time to do them all myself. On top of this are the problems you have with staff: all their dramas, pettiness, in-fighting and personal baggage. Yet in spite of it all I still enjoy what I do.

Acquiring property is very exciting, but once acquired, it becomes another mouth to feed. Rarely are things done right for me, in that I could always do better. Staff and contractors are very difficult to handle: they think they do a fantastic job but are rarely totally committed, and nothing is ever their fault. If they cannot do something they just ignore it and don't notify me; they feel unappreciated and that they are worth far more than they are paid, and that they are indispensable and owed a living. Staff, when you point out their downfalls, become defensive. If you tell them what is needed, they say you are always criticising and never satisfied.

When I had far fewer HMOs, my frustration lay in not having enough staff to do the work I wanted done. Contractors were very variable and mostly poor at their jobs, and even finding any was a difficult task. Now that I have my own team, the job is far easier but nowhere near perfect. I love being able to pick up the phone and ask one of my crew to fix something and knowing that most of the time they will do it. Previously, I would spend hours trying to find someone, then wait for them to turn up to let them into the property. Since I did not know them, I could not trust them by themselves in one of my tenants' properties! I once calculated that a plumber I used only turned up to one in eight appointments – and he was the best I could find at the time!

Most of my satisfaction comes from talking about property. Doing deals is exciting and, looking after properties and tenants is gratifying in moderation.

CHAPTER 9
CAN YOU EVICT UNEMPLOYED TENANTS
WHO REFUSE TO PAY THEIR 'TOP UP'?

Yes, you can evict a tenant if they refuse to pay their 'top up'. Even if the tenants are only £1 in arrears, whether for 'top up' or not you can start the eviction process. 'Top up' is the difference between the rent paid by Housing Benefit and the rent charged. The tenant has to pay this 'top up' from the benefit they receive. I will only evict a tenant if they are a problem and I treat the non-payment of top up as rent arrears, which gives me grounds to evict. I do not usually evict tenants solely because they fail to pay top up as I am still receiving 90% of the rent, and changing a tenant for this is not worth the effort. It is only worth it if the tenant is also causing trouble, and the beauty is that almost all troublesome tenants do not pay their 'top up', which makes it easier to evict them, as getting enough evidence to evict for antisocial behaviour or other grounds can be very difficult. I use the little-known or used 'Ground 10', which states that a landlord can evict if the tenant is in ANY rent arrears. Ground 10 is a discretionary ground, which means the judge has discretion to grant an eviction. In my experience of completing over 350 evictions using the courts, it has never failed; judges will always give a possession order or give a suspended possession order (see below), even though Ground 10 is discretionary.

If the arrears amount to over eight weeks rent arrears at the time you serve notice to evict, you can use the better-known 'Ground 8' notice (eight weeks or more arrears at the time of serving notice *and* at the time of the court hearing). You will automatically obtain possession. You can serve a Ground 8 and 10 together, which catches the tenant who owed eight weeks rent arrears at the time you served the eviction notice, but reduces the arrears to below eight weeks at the court hearing.

I find that once I serve a Ground 8 and or Ground 10 the tenant either starts behaving and agrees to pay up (very rare), or their behaviour deteriorates (usual). I have never had a judge refuse to exercise their discretionary powers or refuse to evict on Ground 10 (the tenants are in arrears but not eight weeks or over), defended or undefended. Most possession cases are undefended, which means the tenant fails to appear, and so the court hearing is in my view a waste of time. If defended, what I always do (and I recommend you do the same) is to agree with the tenant's legal representative, if any, or with the judge that I will accept a suspended possession order. This means the possession is suspended providing the tenant pays their rent and usually a small amount towards their arrears. The tenant rarely pays either.

The judges are in my experience always happy to agree to this arrangement and the legal representatives are too. No one claims at a hearing that they will not pay and won't go until they are over eight weeks in arrears, nor demands that the judge refuse to exercise their discretion not to give possession on Ground 10, i.e. eviction where the tenant is less than eight weeks in arrears. Note: Ground 10 is given at the judge's discretion and judges do not have to give a possession order.

The eviction process looks like a lot of trouble, but once you get used to it, it is easy, and if you follow my system it only takes nine weeks plus the time the bailiff takes to act. See how to evict in nine weeks in my guide *DIY Eviction*. Following the correct legal procedure is a lot better, I can assure you, than defending an action for unlawful eviction as I have done and won to my cost. You can rarely recover your legal costs even if you successfully defend against a tenant who sues you. Either way you pay!

I suggest to always try to negotiate with the tenant before applying for a court possession. In my manual *DIY Eviction*, available from www.hmodaddy.com, I show you how to do this and how to evict within nine weeks. Negotiation is always quicker and cheaper and works most of time if you do it with respect and humour. In conclusion, it will work in your favour to act promptly with bad tenants, as the process can take months and does not start until you serve notice. A bad tenant only becomes worse, so do not delay in acting.

There is a myth that tenants care about their housing, want security and need protection. I can assure you that there are a significant number of tenants who look upon their accommodation as nothing more than a paper handkerchief, a completely disposable object, and have little regard to their obligations as a tenant. Yet the authorities treat all tenants as deserving of the full protection of the one-sided legal process and exercise no discretion when you are dealing with such anti-social tenants.

The unfair system gets worse – some of these tenants realise that they have all the power, and if you as a landlord make one wrong move they will try and exploit the situation they caused to sue you for thousands of pounds using 'no win no fee' solicitors who will gladly do all the work for them. You need to be very careful when dealing with such tenants, as compensation for unlawful eviction starts at around £5k plus legal costs, which are usually a lot more. For more information on unlawful eviction read my book *HMOs and Compensation for Unlawful Eviction* from www.hmodaddy.com. Dealing with such tenants takes great skill, but once you appreciate that tenants have the power and learn to handle them with sensitivity, you can usually get most to see reason and leave without too much trouble or cost.

CHAPTER 10
WHAT IS WRONG WITH HOUSING STANDARDS?

To start with, I would like to state that I am not a supporter or advocate for unsafe or poor-quality housing, but if an owner-occupier can buy and live in a derelict house why can't tenants? Why are all tenants treated as needing special protection? Why can't a tenant rent (which I emphasise it is illegal for a landlord to offer) a substandard property, presumably at a lower rent or other discount, and either the landlord or tenant agree to repair it?

I think everyone would agree that a structurally unsafe

house, rotten floors, holes in the ceiling, roof, windows and floors, bare electric wiring, blocked sewers etc. are all entirely unacceptable and should not be allowed. However, what the Council means by poor quality housing covers a lot more than this, including often trivial things of little or no consequence. It is these, what I consider to be unnecessary extras, that I question.

I strongly suspect that much of the drive to increase standards is not motivated by a concern for tenant welfare but a backdoor way to ban HMOs. Local Authorities are pushed by their councillors, though some housing standards officers are also clearly anti-landlord and are against HMOs. What other type of housing is officially banned – which is what the introduction of Article 4 Directives (which effectively bans HMOs) means. The government removed the need for planning permission for HMOs in 2010, which up until then was the main limiter on the supply of HMOs. I believe some Local Authorities are cynically using the "safety and welfare of tenants" to restrict the supply of HMOs. Appreciate also that failure to comply with these often pointless rules can also mean that the landlord can end up with a criminal conviction or a civil penalty.

In my opinion, government and Local Authority standards have not adapted to the demands and usage of the 21st century. They hark back to the 20th century and I don't know if they had very much relevance even then. For example:

1. **Too high a standard for fire protection:** On any sensible risk analysis there is little need for much fire protection in a small HMO let to non-vulnerable tenants. Even worse, the standards have failed to take account of the best technology, i.e. fire sprinklers. If the over-the-top standards for fire sprinklers were relaxed, then I believe it would be cheaper to fit a sprinkler system than fire doors and so much of the extra fire protection that many Local Authorities demand. To quote the Birmingham Chief Fire Officer:

   'There has never been a death due to fire in a fully sprinkler property.'

   Yet Local Authorities' Housing Standards departments still demand mostly passive fire protection, which for an HMO usually means fire doors and a fire alarm. There is little justification for the standards imposed by many Local Authorities on HMO landlords. The government does not require such a high standard, just 'appropriate fire precautions and equipment', and that is the problem. What is 'appropriate' varies a lot between those who are paying and those who are not. The landlord pays and the Council decides what is needed.

2. **The requirements for cooking facilities:** It is clear to me from 25 years observation and the 10,000-plus tenants that I have housed that nearly all homegrown HMO tenants do not cook. With regard to tenants from

overseas it is very different; they usually like to cook. I suspect that where single people live in flats and houses the same will be found and it is not exclusive to HMO tenants. Local Authorities can't be excused from enforcing the need for cooking facilities, as, by law, licensed HMOs must have a kitchen for every five residents. However, this does not account for the attempt to increase the need for cooking facilities by some Local Authorities, or the excessive space and other standards and requirements for kitchens demanded by some council officers.

Note that there is no need to provide cooking facilities and many of the onerous standards which HMOs must comply with in single-lets. Conversely there is no requirement to furnish an HMO or even supply a bed, yet every tenant I have come across sleeps but very few cook.

3. **The space standards for bedrooms and other facilities**: There is no evidence to show the size of accommodation is in anyway detrimental. The need for space standards in the Private Rented Sector where tenants are free to choose what accommodation size they want and are prepared to pay for is, I submit, up to them. Some tenants use their accommodation just to sleep in; they go home at the weekend and shower and eat at work.

Most Local Authorities demand a minimum of 6.5 sq. metres for a bedroom (some even more) yet we forcibly incarcerate prisoners in cells of 3.2 sq. metres and it is considered humane to be incarcerated in such a space for up to 23 hours a day. People are sent to prison as a punishment, not to be punished. The deprivation of their freedom is considered sufficient punishment and no, I am not saying that tenants should be treated like prisoners, but they should be allowed to choose what they wish to pay for as long as it is not harmful to their wellbeing. Which is better, cheap accommodation or the streets? What about the benefit of having surplus money to spend as you will? By insisting on a minimum space size for rooms the Local Authorities are effectively removing low cost housing from the market. Why they should wish to do this I have never had a sensible answer. Most housing officers retreat to 'My rules say'. They are often frightened to have an opinion.

4. **Gas safety**: This has to be one of the goals of the 20th century. I agree it is appalling that people should die from or be harmed by carbon monoxide poisoning and appropriate steps should be taken to avoid such deaths and harm, but the attempt to prevent carbon monoxide poisoning did not look at the cause and instead resulted in excessive regulation mainly imposed on the rental sector, not on owner-occupied property. The regulations were lapped up by the industry itself, as it created an

enormous amount of extra business to test and supervise gas supplies in tenanted properties, consequently increasing the cost of providing gas in such properties.

The majority of carbon monoxide deaths in residential property are down to flued gas heaters, which extract oxygen from the room and can become lethal when the flue is blocked and there is insufficient ventilation. Most modern boilers and gas fires are of a balanced flue type which takes oxygen from outside. This type is fail-safe if properly installed and rarely causes problems. Nearly all of the problems with gas could be prevented by banning non-balanced flued gas appliances from rented accommodation, or checking only the non-balanced flue types and/or phasing them out, instead of this enormous bureaucratic testing system. The exception is gas cookers: these are un-flued but require a well-ventilated kitchen and are not usually left on. Since October 2015 there has been a requirement to fit and provide a testing regime for carbon monoxide detectors where solid fuel is burnt, again for what I believe to be little discernible benefit.

Many landlords, because of the gas regulations, refuse to install gas or remove it, leaving tenants to use electric heaters which cost a lot more to heat a property with than gas. This has resulted in the need to provide enormous subsidies to encourage landlords to supply gas heating so that low income tenants aren't left with what some consider the choice between freezing or starving to death. It is estimated that about 40 people per year die due to carbon monoxide poisoning, and that the regulations save about 20 lives a year.

Yet compare this to the estimated 30,000 people dying due to cold every year. I appreciate heating is a complex topic and it does not necessarily follow that the cheapest form of heating necessarily turns out cheaper in practice. A lot has to do with lifestyle.

5. **Need for electrical safety certificates**: All HMOs are required to have an Electrical Condition Installation Certificate, which usually lasts five years. The need for electricity testing is I believe of little value on a cost-risk analysis – but who cares, as any cost is pushed on to the landlord! A cost-risk analysis looks at the number of people killed or injured compared to the cost of prevention, in this case the cost of testing and upgrading the installation to meet current standards compared to the number of injuries and lives saved. This cost-risk analysis was not carried out before or after the introduction of electrical safety certificates. I also suspect strongly that if a cost benefit analysis was carried out it would find very little benefit and certainly not be worth the cost. Again, jobs for the boys at the landlord's expense.

It may seem strange to an outsider that when councils introduce licensing schemes their justification for doing so is usually to improve the quality of housing, yet the first thing they demand is gas and electricity certificates along with the fee and a completed application form, and often very little else. As I have explained, these certificates achieve very little and just raise the landlord's costs, so you may now appreciate why I find it difficult to understand what poor quality housing means and how licensing is going to eliminate it.

6. **Energy efficiency:** This is going to be one of the unrecognised mis-selling scandals of the decade and I doubt it will ever be exposed and the guilty punished. The knowledge and understanding of energy efficiency is known to those who have created a business trying to sell us their products that they allege can save us money, so they are hardly likely to admit it does not work or only works in theory.

Scientists and governments need to look to their own consciences on this – I fail to understand why the truth has not come out. Why are consumer organisations not speaking out? There has been the occasional news writer, mainly in the Daily Mail, who has questioned energy efficiency, a bit like the mis-selling of financial products before it became fully exposed, but little more. All very strange.

I would very much like to save money and the planet so I have tried a few of the remedies and probably unlike most, tested or monitored the results in the over 140 properties for which I pay utilities. With over 140 properties I am in an almost unique position to compare costs on such a large scale, and I am sorry to report that I can find little evidence to support any savings from the limited experimentation I have undertaken. I have fitted new condensing boilers and extra roof and wall insulation, and found little difference in energy usage. I have not tried products which are said to reduce costs by less than 10%, as it would be almost impossible for me to detect such a small saving. Nor have I tested products which give a return of less than about 20%, as the cost saving is not viable for me.

If a landlord wishes to save on electricity usage then they should fit pre-pay electricity meters to each room. I do this by paying for the electrical supply to the HMO and fitting pre-pay secondary meters to each room where I resell electricity to the tenants. I have found that this in itself causes the amount of electricity used in the house to drop by 48% on average. When the electricity is included in the rent I find tenants leave an enormous number of electrical items switched on. As soon as pre-pay electricity meters are fitted, where tenants have to pay for the electricity they use, there is a dramatic change in behaviour. Everything is switched off in their room. The use of electricity meters and shopping around for the cheapest supplier are the only ways I have so far found to save on utility usage.

7. **The need for housing standards departments:** This government is hell bent on imposing financial responsibility on the most vulnerable in our society, those on benefits, by insisting on direct payment of housing benefit to the tenant. Why draw a line at financial responsibility? Why not let the tenants also have responsibility for their own choices in deciding the standard of property to take? They generally have this choice in nearly every other aspect of their lives.

The main criticism of housing standards departments from landlords is that they spend most of their time dealing with generally decent landlords who engage with them and rarely bother to go after the bad landlords, saying they do not have the time or resources to do so. They pick on the good landlords who may have broken some technical rule and will often over-enforce against them. This complaint can be levelled against all law enforcement, not just housing standards departments, as there is no reasonableness or proportionality defence to a crime. All law is equally enforceable and there is nothing to stop an enforcement agency arbitrarily enforcing it, which is entirely within its discretion. So you have to question why some councils enthusiastically enforce some housing standards and ignore other areas when there is no other justification than 'it is the law'!

The vulnerable in society have more than ample opportunity to enforce their rights against landlords with 'no win no fee' solicitors, Citizens Advice Bureaus and other sources, so why do they need a housing standards department to look after them? For the record, and in case any of the housing standards officers I deal with read this, apart from a few notable exceptions housing standards officers I have come across generally try to do a good job in helping tenants and landlords and often act as an unappreciated arbitrator between tenants, other departments and landlords. It's a role I am at times very grateful for and I certainly would not rather deal with 'no win no fee' solicitors. However, the situation is that I have to deal with both.

With Housing Standards, most of the time I get an email from them saying that a tenant has complained about something and my reply is, 'I have already fixed it' or 'I didn't know about it so why did the tenant not report it to me, but I will get it fixed,' and that is the end of the matter. The Housing Standards department's intervention was unnecessary – just tell the tenant to report it to their landlord. Any decent landlord will act on a tenant's complaint. Most of the complaints to the Council from my tenants are submitted by those who want to be re-housed in the social sector and, I strongly suspect, are trying to claim that their current living conditions are bad in order to obtain priority for social housing. I can understand this, as often the social sector provides, due to the enormous subsidies they receive or did receive, better or cheaper housing, and the tenant has the right to buy the property at a massive discount. Social Housing needs tenants if they have voids and I have found that they will often encourage my tenants to leave my accommodation in order to join them.

Housing Standards officers are one of the many contributors to creating homelessness. What Housing Standards officers seem to fail to appreciate is that any business has to be viable, and even if I put aside my 'what is the use' argument about the standards that they try to impose, there is a commerciality argument. Can a landlord provide housing of the standard required at an affordable rent? The answer is often no. So where do the tenants who cannot afford the rent go? Housing Standards officers don't care where they go since that is neither their problem nor department. The answer used to be Social Housing, yet no one makes the connection that the social sector can only afford to provide housing of a particular standard as they receive, or did receive, substantial subsidies to do so.

It often costs over ten times what private landlords receive as the market rent and sometimes more to house

HMO tenants within the social sector. I believe this money would have been far better spent encouraging the private sector to provide housing, since it does so far more cheaply. Social housing is no longer going to be an option as funding is being reduced to the social sector. The result is that people are made homeless, or if they want a home tenants are given no option but to live where housing is affordable, which is mainly in the North of England.

I believe that one of the reasons that landlords and landlord associations do not highlight the above issues with Housing Standards is that it is not in their best interests. Landlords want standards and enforcement to be draconian as long as it is not against them personally, but is used to deter other potential landlords as it discourages them or makes it too expensive to consider letting a vacant property. Landlords want to reduce competition, not encourage it. Imagine the flood of properties that would become available if the restrictions on standards were lifted!

Conclusion

The above is only a small sample of requirements imposed on HMO landlords for no or very little benefit on either a risk basis or cost-benefit analysis to both the tenant and landlord. These requirements create substantial cost for the landlord in providing, checking and maintaining such requirements and increase the chance of pushing the landlord into the risk of criminal sanctions for failure to comply, often for nothing more than unintended lapse or ignorance of said provisions.

It is unfortunate that there is no analysis of housing standards; it is just a hotchpotch of rules thrown together over decades at the whim of whoever is in government, and enforced at the discretion of Local Authorities. Unfortunately this is true of so many other sectors and there is no science or evaluation to most legislation. If one compares legislation to the practice of medicine, law-making and enforcement are medieval, far worse than witchcraft.

MASTER HMO'S TODAY,
CHANGE YOUR LIFE
FOREVER

BOOKS

MANUALS

COURSES

MENTORSHIPS

AND CONSULTANCY

AVAILABLE FROM HMO DADDY
at WWW.HMODADDY.COM

BOOKS

HMO Landlord Rules – £4.99

Downloadable version – £1.99

Written by an HMO landlord with 20 years' experience, this small, frank and helpful guide looks at exactly what works and what doesn't when managing properties. Instilled with a strong sense of evidence and proof, the author exposes some widely-accepted claims as rubbish or a con. The aim is to ensure maximum income for minimum work. It includes helpful information such as: • How to pick good tenants and get rid of bad ones • Whether to believe non-payment excuses • When to give something for free and when to charge • When to serve notice on a tenant • How to deal with abandonment and late payments • How to avoid litigation • And much more!

HMO Daddy Reveals All – £19.99
(Published April 2017)

Downloadable version – £14.99

Jim Haliburton (HMO Daddy) reveals all in this easy-to-read, comprehensive guide. The publication details Jim's extensive knowledge on all aspects of the HMO market. Aimed at both existing HMO landlords and those who are thinking about entering the market alike, Jim discusses the problems and issues surrounding what can be a complex investment.

This HMO business can be a lonely road, with seemingly no one to turn to who is able to understand the problems we encounter – Jim's guide helps investors through these difficulties with this much-needed clarity and candour, as is Jim's inimitable style.

101 Questions & Answers Relating to HMOs – £9.99

Downloadable version – £6.93

All the questions you wanted answers to and some you had not even thought about. Jim Haliburton, also known as the HMO Daddy, has compiled the answers to the questions he has been asked. There is an enormous thirst for knowledge about HMOs from existing HMO landlords and those thinking of entering the business, and HMO Daddy has not shirked away from answering even the most difficult of them. A must-read for all those who have HMOs or are thinking about becoming an HMO landlord.

More 101 Questions & Answers Relating to HMOs – £9.99

Downloadable version – £6.93

In this book, Jim Haliburton answers even more of the essential questions you had about HMOs including his personal property journey, how to get started on your HMO journey, potential tenant issues, how to let to the unemployed or homeless, dealing with utilities, handling general HMO issues, matters regarding the authorities prosecuting landlords and HMO funding techniques.

35 Money Making or Saving Tips for HMO Landlords – £9.99

Downloadable version – £6.93

Written by an experienced HMO landlord, this is an insider's guide to creating extra income and savings from your property portfolio. It includes information to help you make savings on repairs, maintenance and decoration of your properties. It includes tried and tested tips used by the author himself, and includes information on creating extra rooms in your properties, introducing and charging extra fees and top-ups, fitting master locks and electricity meters and making savings on light fittings, repairs and decoration. It explains which services can be charged for and which should be free, as well as how and when to introduce new fees without upsetting your tenants. If you're an HMO landlord this will give you a frank and honest way to maximise the returns on your property. Just applying FIVE of the tips to four of your HMOs will give you the PROFIT of an EXTRA HMO.

Planning & HMOs – £9.99

Downloadable version – £6.93

HMO landlords provide low-cost, flexible housing desperately needed by society, often to vulnerable tenants. However, they are rarely given help or support by the authorities and the law is often vigorously enforced against them. Little is said about the damage some tenants cause to property, problems with rent arrears and the eviction of bad tenants. This book is for the brave souls who dare to provide HMO housing and need a guide to the planning system. It shows you how to stand up to councils that try to stop you providing good quality HMO accommodation. If you stand up to the planners, you will be surprised how rarely they will follow through and how often they will lose. A unique insight into and practical information about planning rules and planning appeals for shared houses and multi-lets by an experienced HMO landlord.

HMO & Compensation for Unlawful Eviction – £9.99

Downloadable version – £6.93

This practical, down-to-earth guide is written by HMO Daddy, an experienced landlord who had a case brought against him for unlawful eviction by an HMO tenant. When he got to court, he realised he was looking at a possible compensation claim of around £100,000. With no experience in this area, he could find little guidance or help to explain the system. He won his case – but this is the book he wishes he'd had at the time! This quick and easy-to-understand guide examines court reports and cases involving unlawful eviction along with the amount of compensation awarded. It brings home to landlords the seriousness of the risks they are taking when evicting tenants, and more importantly it explains how to avoid ending up in court.

A Compendium of HMO Daddy's Blogs – £4.99 self-published

Downloadable version – £1.93

This collection of invaluable HMO advice and tips shared by Jim Haliburton covers tips for new investors into HMOs, costly mistakes to avoid, how to become a successful HMO investor, what makes a property investor different from a general investor, how to avoid LHA claims, unusual properties bought, how to evict unemployed tenants who refuse to pay and what is wrong with current housing standards.

Current Issues for HMO Landlords – £9.99 self-published

Downloadable version – £6.93

Current issues for HMO Landlords looks at the twelve pressing issues in detail that landlords or property investors frequently ask about, including which properties let and which ones do not, whether to use AST or licences for HMOs, how to keep tenants, assessing rent to rent, getting commercial finance, when to fix and when not to fix a mortgage, how to save money on heating, when to use letting agents and when not to, as well as how to identify the need for HMOs.

Introduction to Letting to the Unemployed – £9.99 self-published

Downloadable version – £6.93

This is probably the most heartfelt book I have ever written, as it deals with homelessness, and I have been homeless myself when I left care as a child. I have given numerous copies away to the lovely people I meet who tell me they want to start an HMO to house the homeless, women who have been domestically abused and the like. Please read it before you start to let to the unemployed, and I applaud and will help you if you decide to go ahead.

Serviced Accommodation – £9.99 self-published

Downloadable version – £6.93

This book is an outline of the legalities involved in operating as Serviced Accommodation. I wrote this because when I first considered using some of my properties for Serviced Accommodation I could not find any information on the subject. I, therefore, researched the topic and have come up with this book.

Employing an HMO Manager
(to be published end of 2017)

Jim Haliburton, known as the HMO Daddy, outlines the process for and nuances in employing a property manager to help efficiently run, systemise and scale the process of running your HMO portfolio.

**To order any book or books please visit
www.hmodaddy.com**

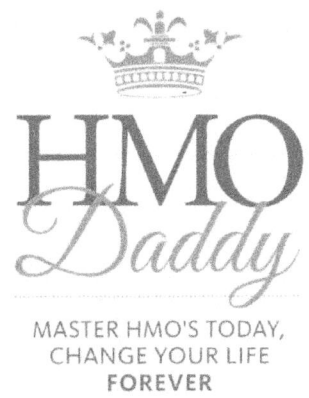

MASTER HMO'S TODAY,
CHANGE YOUR LIFE
FOREVER

MANUALS

How to become a Multi-Millionaire HMO Landlord –
£597

Downloadable version – £497

Written by an experienced HMO landlord with 140 properties and nearly 1000 rooms, originally written in 2005 and updated regularly, this manual stands the test of time and is the authoritative guide to starting and setting up an HMO. The manual shows how HMO Daddy started and runs his HMOs and how you can do the same. It covers the HMO market, acquiring the ideal property for an HMO, negotiating the right price, tenant selection, property management, property standards and general advice on property. The *How to become a Multi-Millionaire Landlord* manual will help novice or experienced single-let landlords transform their property portfolios into profitable multi-million-pound cash-flowing assets. A complete how-to guide in one manual.

DIY Eviction – £125

Downloadable version – £99

Jim Haliburton (HMO Daddy) uses his experience of evicting over 300 tenants through the courts with 100% success, and far more tenants without having to go court to evict, to show that by using the correct legal process it is possible to evict a problem tenant without the necessity of using a lawyer. This is the only DIY guide to evicting tenants and explains simply how to evict tenants, and if they refuse to go, how to use the legal process to successfully remove them from your property cheaply, quickly, easily and legally. The guide tells you how to answer all the questions ever asked of Jim by judges in the eviction process and how to deal with things when the eviction goes wrong. It is recommended you buy this along with the book *HMOs and Compensation for Unlawful Eviction* (see book section).

Operating Standards – £297

Downloadable version – £197

Operating Standards contains all the knowledge, the scripts, the tools and the systems to run your HMO portfolio, with clear step-by-step processes to manage any potential HMO issues.

The thought of starting or running an HMO portfolio can be very daunting as you do not know whose advice you can trust, how to get the legalities of letting to tenants right, or the issues involved in inspecting properties.

Operating Standards contains all the information you need to run your HMO and consistently build your income including customer care, letting criteria and arranging interviews, answering the telephone to prospective clients, showing premises, handing over premises, tenant rating, repairs and tenant requests, dealing with tenants, dealing with local housing allowance (LHA) claimants, dealing with late paying tenants, collection of rents and dealing with building works and renovations.

Implementing these operating standards has the potential to replace your salary in 12 months and contains plans and checklists to help you run your HMO efficiently and profitably, or show staff how to do it.

Forms, Notices, Agreements and Manuals with memory stick – £225

Downloadable version – £125

The Forms, Notices and Agreements manual covers all the relevant forms including application forms for tenants, tenancy pack, abandonment documentation, ASTs, Court forms and assorted notices for tenants including Section 8, Ground 8, Ground 10 & Ground 11 for landlords – 65 different forms, notices and agreements at the last count.

These forms, lists, notices and agreements are essential paperwork that all beginner or established landlords must have to run their property portfolios legally, efficiently and profitably.

To order a manual or manuals please visit:
www.hmodaddy.com

COURSES

Tour of HMOs – £297 One-Day Course

Our famous Tour of HMOs day is a behind-the-scenes look at how Jim Haliburton sets up and runs his HMOs. The day will give you an incredible insight into how you can maximise profit whilst still offering the very best in tenant care and safety! Jim houses over 1000 tenants and has all types of properties throughout the West Midlands area.

During your one-day course you will be taken to visit several different HMOs, including 2 and 3 bedroom terraced or semi-detached houses that are now 5 or 6 bed HMOs.

You will be shown how to maximise the income from a typical single let from a gross of **£550 pcm** to a phenomenal **£3120 pcm** gross from the same property converted to an HMO, all legally and ethically.

Come and learn from my over 26 years of property investing experience about how I acquire, set up, convert, refurbish and manage the 140 HMOs in my portfolio with in excess of 900 rooms, and still counting.

Whether you are an experienced property investor or are thinking about investing in property, HMO investment is definitely the way forward to maximise your rental returns. Over 2500 people have now attended HMO Daddy's Tour of HMOs – probably the most popular HMO course ever! Come and see first-hand exactly what an HMO is by visiting several of my HMOs with me.

- The course includes:
- All the course materials and slides
- Expert tuition with the HMO Daddy team
- Transport to and from the HMOs – we aim to visit up to 3 properties in various stages of conversion
- Lunch
- Tea and coffee breaks
- Overnight stay in one of HMO Daddy's HMOs (subject to pre-booking and availability).

Commercial to Residential £1997 Two Day Course

In every town in the UK there are old, empty, unloved units gathering dust. Have you ever looked and thought 'I wonder if I could turn that giant building into profit somehow?'

You can, and we want to show you, right away, how to acquire such a property for £1 or less, and how to finance so that you can obtain and recover all you spend on the property so that you do NOT NEED MONEY to acquire such properties.

Covering all the legislation and conversion considerations you need to know, we also take a tour of several converted premises to show you what we have done and that you can do it too.

Our unique training programme will provide you with a chance to make a great profit through converting commercial property into cash-flowing residential developments. It takes you through a step-by-step process and shows you how to take control of empty commercial properties with little or no money at all and convert them into profitable residential premises.

This course will cover among other things how to easily identify commercial to residential conversion opportunities, understanding planning laws and loopholes, putting your team together, and getting other people to fund the conversion process if required.

Rent to Rent – £397 One Day Course

Do you know the difference between a rent to rent deal, a rent to buy deal, a lease option, an instalment contract, and an exchange with delayed completion?

You have heard these terms bandied around the industry for a few years but you have not yet found anyone who can clarify the difference and show you which of these strategies is right for you.

This is where I come in. There are very subtle differences in these strategies, but all of them are within reach even if you have very little capital to invest, as shown by HMO Daddy, who walks the talk and who has over 30 rent-to-rents.

This introduction is perfect for you if you are starting out on your rent to rent journey.

Learn the basics of deal sourcing and negotiation. The course provides you with the paperwork to go out and immediately make rent-to-rent contacts.

Come armed and ready to develop your understanding of rent to rent. Discover how you can kick-start your rent to rent business straight away.

For a small investment of just £397 (no VAT) you can join us with a guest FREE OF CHARGE and kick-start your journey to financial freedom.

The HMO Success Formula – £1997 Two-Day Course

This two-day course provides a step-by-step guide on how to become an HMO landlord whether you are a novice or experienced landlord.

Designed by Jim Haliburton the HMO Daddy, this course covers all the relevant information required to enable you to succeed in setting up and efficiently running your portfolio of HMO properties for great profit. It includes comprehensive course notes.

COURSE CONTENT

Income from HMOs

HMO Licencing

Objection to HMOs

Different Models of HMOs

HMO Hot Spots

Attracting Tenants

Interviewing Tenants

Keeping Tenants

HMO Strategies including:

Buying

Rent-to-Rent

Delayed Completion

Vendor Finance

Leases

Commercial to Residential

Adverse Possession

What Is an HMO

HMO Myths

How HMOs Are Valued

Different Models of HMOs

Finding Tenants

Managing HMOs

Planning

Council Tax

Utility Costs – How To Reduce and Avoid

Tenant Issues

Building Control

Housing Standards

Conversion Costs

With all courses, you can stay on HMO Daddy's HMO rooms for a nominal charge subject to availability and prior booking

The courses are usually held at our training suite in Walsall

To book a course or courses please go to: www.hmodaddy.com

MENTORSHIPS

HMO Academy
Work as an HMO Landlord – free of charge

The HMO Academy 400-hour internship – come to us in Walsall for 400 hours over about six months (an average of a couple of days per week), or you can do it all in one go, which should take you around 8 weeks – you choose how you want to do it. Shadowing every department of our lettings company, you get a chance to assist with tenant interviews, viewings, rent collection, maintenance, and house conversion, and also spend time with the HMO Daddy training team acquiring new properties and planning their conversion.

By attending the HMO Daddy Academy, you will receive the extensive course manual and our operating standards which you are expected to read and understand. You will learn all the techniques you need to run your own portfolio and spend a lot of quality time with Jim Haliburton and the team....in return we ask you to work as requested in the various departments and bring whatever skills you have to the business. To apply we ask for your CV or a summary of you and what you have done, some personal details and a deposit of £1200. When you complete the 400 hours we return the £1200 deposit. Free accommodation is available.

HMO Daddy offers limited bursaries for the above. If you are unable to afford the £1200 deposit you can apply for a bursary to cover the deposit, your travel and subsistence.

MASTER HMO'S TODAY,
CHANGE YOUR LIFE
FOREVER

HMO Mastery-Mentorship Program – £7,999 for the full 12 months (extension is available) or £3,200 plus £500 pcm payable by S.O.

Property training is a fantastic way to extend your knowledge and learn what to do and what not to do. But how many times have you attended a training day and got home full of good intentions to change your world, only to lose momentum the following day, week, month?

To keep you focused and continually moving forwards in your journey, HMO Daddy has carefully crafted the 12 Month Mastery programme, which will provide you with ongoing training, coaching and support for the next 12 months of your property journey.

The Mastery programme is designed to encourage you to think outside of your natural capabilities. It will push you to the next level and most importantly it will keep you accountable in both a group setting and individually.

During each monthly session held 1-4pm at our Wednesbury

office on the first Tuesday of the month (excluding August and December), you will work to develop your business and goals, analyse your deals, and discuss your challenges with the HMO Daddy team and the other Mastery members. We will then review your activity every month so the grass never grows under your feet and you can be accountable for your own progress. You can ask questions to people who have already done what you are thinking of doing, which will help you to make the right choices to achieve the best results.

The first step of our Mastery programme is a one-to-one session with Jim Haliburton to plan your 12-month journey and set goals to get you started. He will be able to keep things realistic and he will push you to think creatively and break through your own ceiling.

In addition to these interactive sessions you have access to unlimited deal analysis with the HMO Daddy team. You can call the team at any time for advice, help and 'crunching the numbers', and you will receive our exclusive spreadsheet that allows you to analyse your own deals at any time. You also have unlimited access to the HMO Daddy team any time you need advice or support throughout your 12-month journey.

As if all of that was not enough, all of our Mastery members also get the following for no extra charge:

- The HMO Daddy Business in A Bag – 4 operational manuals to set up your HMO business – cost £1,395

- 6 books authored by Jim Haliburton – cost £54.55

- Entry to all of the HMO Daddy courses throughout the 12 months – FOC – costs over £5,000

- Inner Circle Membership – Facebook community and monthly tips and tricks and all webcasts

- Option to spend 3 full days in the J9 lettings part of the business to learn the intricacies of this business – cost £795

- First refusal on JV deals

- Access to the HMO Daddy Power Team - legal, financial, maintenance – priceless

One-to-One Consultations – phone or face-to-face

Telephone or face-to-face consultation. Are you too busy or not inclined to attend a course or just don't know where to start? Then you can have a one-to-one consultation with HMO Daddy or one of HMO Daddy's consultants.

With HMO Daddy	With HMO Daddy's Consultant
½ Hour Fee - **£150**	½ Hour Fee - **£75**
1 Hour Fee - **£250**	1 Hour Fee - **£125**
Half-Day Fee - **£800**	Half-Day Fee - **£400**
Full-Day Fee - **£1400**	Full-Day Fee - **£700**

www.ingramcontent.com/pod-product-compliance
Lightning Source LLC
Chambersburg PA
CBHW070050210526
45170CB00012B/640